Return *to a*
Place *like*
Seeing

Return *to a* Place *like* Seeing

poems

John Palmer

Pleasure Boat Studio
New York

Return to a Place Like Seeing, by John Palmer

ISBN 978-1-929355-08-2
Library of Congress Control Number: 2013914813
First U.S. Printing

Design by Susan Ramundo
Cover by Lauren Grosskopf from *Shelter from the Storm*, a painting
  by Laurie Goddard

Our books are available through your favorite bookstore and through
**SPD (Small Press Distribution), Partners/West, Baker & Taylor,
Ingram, Brodart, Amazon.com,** and **bn.com**

and also through our website via credit card:
PLEASURE BOAT STUDIO: A LITERARY PRESS
www.pleasureboatstudio.com
201 West 89th Street
New York, NY 10024

Contact **Jack Estes**
Fax: 413-677-0085
Email: pleasboat@nyc.rr.com

for SUZANNE
and
for MY PARENTS

ACKNOWLEDGMENTS

American Poets and Poetry: "Original Sin"
American Writing: "Progress"
Antioch Review: "Reserve"
Ascent: "Exchange," "Naked Person's Song"
Chaminade: "Knowing the Days"
Cimarron Review: "Attachments"
Connecticut River Review: "Fast, Faster," "Day of Small Consolations,"
   "Return to a Place Like Home"
Denver Review: "First Stepping in the Deerfield"
Defined Providence: "Reconvening" (published as "Self-Portrait as Water")
Greensboro Review: "The Snow Is No Memory"
High Plains Review: "These Afternoons"
Indiana Review: "Houses by Cézanne"
Nimrod: "All the Time," "Damned," "Land-Holder's Lament"
Northwest Review: "Circle," "Trade and Transport"
Osiris: "Double Time," "Elysian," "Memory Songs," "State"
Phoebe: "Reminded of Former Habits"
Poet Lore: "Evidence," "Rising Sense"
Seneca Review: "Fireflies," "Little Low Earth," "Motion Notes"
Talking River Review: "After Haying," "Current"
Willow Review: "Cistern"
Willow Springs: "Goal"

"Motion Notes" appeared in *Anthology of Magazine Verse and Yearbook of American Poetry* (1997). Some of these poems also appeared in *Open Gate*, an anthology of Deerfield poets.

CONTENTS

I

MOTION NOTES

ATTACHMENTS

The fog burns up and stones,
black, big as cows, shine in the meadow.
A cow's rubbed her throat raw on the fence.
A tuft of hide and blood, damp star,

spangles the wire. Flies in eccentric
orbits envelop our heads. We know
our hair smells like honey, essence
of flowers, the sweet side of decay,

dying and all that. I know you,
always rushing ahead, without realizing,
wanting to be done, your being done
the gravity that pulls me along.

This meadow could shine to the earth's
very brink, but like any ambition
you'd come back the same. Burning,
too material not to return.

EVIDENCE

All week the curtains have bellied in.
Shadows climb past the window,
      and each afternoon one strays
    inside, across the narrow sill,

    a girl with a querying, soft tread
approaching her infant brother,
      too pretty, she thinks, to be a boy,
    his face too lively with sleep to trouble.

    Someone has oiled the good oak trunk
under the window, left statice,
      snapdragons, a fan
    of thank-you notes on the bed,

    as if it were late July,
and the afternoons still brilliant, full
      of elms and their low speech
    like a river's. Withdrawing, a shadow

    is the consternation of woods,
of riverbanks, like the misgivings
      in a wise, dark-eyed, immortal sister
    at the evidence of change—the light

    as it finds out listless rooms,
stubborn features on a landscape,
      as it sets each in a motion that is,
    as first, the motion of something else.

FIRST STEPPING IN THE DEERFIELD

It is cool like a passage out of hours.
The dark channel, neither playful nor menacing,
cleaves to the far bank, away from sand, this beach of little,
    dappled girls and their cries.

It is cool in its insistence on speed,
the swifts like cobbles lightly submerged in glass.
It is serious and abstract in its one obligation.

For affection, it has the underside of the sky,
the paler, uneasy underside of willows shirring in thought.
It has the faults of the valley, its lamentations and white scars.

Vault of winds in its eye,
score of hawk-whistle and plain-chanting, up-water dams in its past,
it bows out to us, sheering our ankles and racing.

Time told by the rope swing's arc,
body in space, frozen a beat,
River, receive us, wading, asquint in this green sun.

ORIGINAL SIN

The sun's still low, catching its breath.
A neighbor's music crawls,
voice first, along the street, under
a rumble left over from last night's storm.

Last night, I woke and my three-day fever
had lifted with its dream—
sweated over and over again like guilt—
of card players
exchanging white, ribboned bundles.

In the yard, where the willow
dangles from heaven,
is a storm-toss of sticks and the thin,
browned fingers of the tree, broken
as if for wanting to be alone.

I hope it will be cool this morning,
like islands beneath an airplane,
and, after all, no voices,
only these ragged clouds
and a blue sky like a shiver.

I'd wanted to be alone,
a small room close to the treetops,
the only words needed
on a day unimpressed by any sound
but the slap of blinds against a sill.

And though the day was as quiet as that,
as the start of a deliberate separation,
I was already wishing myself away,
in other houses, warmer company.

LOVE TRIANGLE

The air particulates. For early evening's memory's
sake, it bluely atomizes,
furring the sun to orange blotch, and blunts
its points on east, on river, on wishes,

ever only abject, flung like Quikshops through
the suburbs. While space fills in,
bluer yet, to be pricked by candlelight, I've
an hour on either side of me and gangs of whispers,

loiterers, angers in my chest. Our old fox
trots past, home, along the fence, some flicky
catch bearding his jaw and only
the dampening ground between him and rest

in the raspberries' roots. Just so far
along the rise then down to the easy curl of body
in its den, the physical dark
pulled close around, and wishes become

instant in his mouth—warm, forgettable, whole.
An hour on either side but this moment
like pieces in my hands, an object,
objects to be shelved, closeted, and only after years

displayed, as "Dying Day," "Cheaper
Self," "The Start of Horror." You,
you and I, and I of a hundred insufficient eyes,
bluely watchful, jittery, little beard.

ONSET

He sniffs ammonia,
the third time in a week, remembers
waving as her taxi pulsed,

once, at the corner
then bore into the tide of traffic.
The night freight crosses the sky,

its nightmares of coal
careening toward a city's mountain
of cold. A cricket skitters

across the alarm clock's
digital welts, as if cellophane
bunched in his head were crackling

open. His hands buzz,
sizzle like crossed wires, flare white into
each iris. He can't sleep. Heart

races to keep up,
as if the roar tonight were just love.

NAKED PERSON'S SONG

I've come as far as my warmth will take me.
Now, someone grinding wind
blows my hiding place in the hedge apart.

A bird drops feathers; the philanthropic
trees of the boulevard drop leaves.
I weave a little boa, beg a paper

from the newsboy with spiky hair,
and, there, I'm clad again, an advertisement
for a vacation in the Islands.

So, I come to sun and surf and snorkel
in their tepid, pearl-colored bays,
as if I were someone with a billfold.

All the while, brick by brick,
my little house gets hauled away to build a jail.
I would visit you there, old life,

bring you cakes and magazines.
It wasn't to be so far from you. I left
thinking I couldn't be missed.

RESERVE

The Outer Banks, N.C.

So many fish, such hoopla flashing ashore
in sequins, then spinning and crowding around
the fishermen's waders. Red pick-ups roar
by themselves, coffee in their pipes, fouling
the hot, gull-tinctured dunes above the beach.

The Cape's out of its head with March contentment.
Its Orpheus is strumming somewhere, levitating
the spirits of winter-thinking water and scrub,
the loblollies in anguish over carving sleet.
Even the horizon, blue lips, cracks with joy.

Camellias, paper wrappers, litter the grass
just inland where benignly his song goes to work.
I'm engineering a complex of dams and alternate
channels to steer the ebb into a black puddle.

Kites and school children flit in the air, down
and into the future from the hill at Kitty Hawk.
Old hands razzle up fish, glistening iron
straight from the water. Be glad winter's dead
and the sky boils to fame, wise storms, new guests:

That's his song. He turned to her, of course,
because he didn't want her, sent her glimmering
back to the dead. But you, flesh, O far-away-bones,
why make me wait?

A DEED INSTEAD OF KNOWING

Mad or not, sad or not, rapacious,
concupiscent or not, indigent or not,
curious, clever, keen or not,
glad but bored or not, boring
your lonesome bit into any
handy mind or not, a cry,
a straggle of destitution wending,
snaking, weaving (or not) its way along
the river valley, moonlit alleys
you call memory, cold history,
that collective—*what?*—its quantum,
common stuff that owes
its twenty-eight essential, sane
irruptions to God or not, God!
or not, forsaken, shaken,
taken to the flecked and very edge
of galaxy and continent and love
and me, who doesn't know,
and can't, the single way for you
of words and sends instead this and not
reproof, not proof, but maybe plea.

STATE

They are thoughts, mechanical as wings.
No one stops here anymore
except to find a room for sleep.
But the sounds go up and down, again, like wings.

When night comes, it fills the body with bees.
My last great adventure was over
the mountains struck from snow-blue metal
and, since, only versions of the local utterance.

I've lost myself, the other voice of things.
I could stay, try to sleep,
let even these few, thin,
recurrent thoughts fade like statues.

They say, "There's a calamity that attracts the iron."
That's a false translation but for its sound . . .
Stinging like rust,
spread through all the ill-used valves.

ATTENTION'S BRIEF

Nothing's final, even the ice,
even the day's lovely heart slicked
with time and what rare event,
like two children skating across
the river and soft into a bank
of quiet. But nothing begins,
and with an air of home, around
a cradle of melting logs, their embers
tremulous as a thing underwater.
I watch, temporarily, as dusk
continues up the valley in a gray
elation, a gray, serene song.
In a wind like a humming, wind
like one erasing with light hand.

ELYSIAN

The sun at four's still dead overhead,
and someone clever's playing *The Firebird*.

The women of the boulevard are wrapped in gauze,
their narrow shoes like masons' hammers

tapping past this prostrate cafe.
A street crew's sawhorse winks a warning amber.

From the manhole, a black man's hand
motions for its spirit level, and bikers

just beyond the hole are bent by waves
of exhaust. Lovers in the awning's shade

lean their heads together but speak
in hands. They say the wind has ribbons

it passes through the broken places in a heart.
I let small coins splatter in a saucer,

have the man with the little linen towel
direct the quick way through the diesel air.

GOAL

A roar in Spanish rises
    from the party downstairs,
        carries a glittering whistle

like birdsong with it, past
    my window. Someone from
        someone else's country

has scored a goal on television.
    Black, importunate clouds
        are reaching from the north.

Across the way, a woman
    clatters utensils in her sink.
        Naked, she slips a taste

of something between her lips,
    stares as if, instead, the dusk
        were softening to peach, here,

in the heart of our courtyard.
    The tv keeps up its ecstatic
        cackling. No one's cat

visits for her dish of milk,
    comes like the silver pulse
        inside a thunderhead.

RECONVENING

Now, like the overall rose and alternate
          lap and run of the sea off Matinicus,

     you have an encompassing look, a catch in your breathing
               that signals the sunrise.

You speak of it coolly, pointedly,
          so that surfaces know their flash.

     You are brackish, persuasive as tide
               or the salt-stickled breeze

as it twines past the lobster boats
          riding their own reflections,

     as it curves through pilings,
               across the mussel-flats.

Each in a fit of balance,
          the gulls spiral inside their own shadows,

     over the one, long shadow
               of which you are the edge and impression.

LONG SHADOWS

They are, really, only circumstances
of a generous calm, of a low, gold
mood like a wine's. We watch them
swaying and crowded in front of

the vaporous sun like hours crawling
toward the hills, like a lake's blue jetties.
The radio is full of poverty,
then of sweet, bookish absences

so that the air might hiss and fatten
and the winsome leaves of the maples
draw attention to their minute
responsiveness, their green agility.

We're in this too, we're meant to say
and promise, afterwards,
to reach a slender arm out
not to hold, but as a sign of having

needed privacy, comprehension, help.
And, shortly, the moon will be under
their sway and smile, only crookedly,
at something in particular—you

and me, which is like one thing, one,
in a day blistered into so many
discrete enmities—you and me,
then a silence like evening, following.

EXCHANGE

There's the gray tide shuddering out and later
          the mud, blue-silver in its flats,
     collecting needles of first sunlight.

     Farther down the inlet, cars flash
along the iron swing-bridge. Each crossing sounds
          like breath across a bottle's mouth.

The leaves nicker like bones or chips of glass,
          like those hard, morning voices
     that are first in the market, exchanging

     forecasts of marriage for the latest
signs of divorce. A heron wades
          along the Indian dam, fixes his eyes

on the repeating rocks. Marginal enterprise
          of stalk and snatch, he's silent from here.
     In a lobster boat's wash, a channel buoy

     taps out its irregular silver time.
The motor thrums through circles of light on the water,
          coins from a maker of half-potent wishes.

HOUSES BY CÉZANNE

The road swings south of the dusty houses,
slopes past outcropped mules to the sculpted fruit
of orchards by the coast, to flowers whose essence
rides like gold-green oil in cruets, to the sea.

Nobody built these houses.
                              They came like geometry:
some air pumped with a blue, evening light, made
voluminous by the crunch of shadows.
                              What's gray
is linear. What's green is a possible life apart,

a breathless step down from the street to a flat
with cobalt bowls, long-stemmed tables, and lemons.
She drew his hand clenched around a lemon, signed
the sheet "DuToit." Pressed fists against his eyes.

What's white curves like the opening of a prayer.
Nobody's waited for. The farmer in his wagon
said the hills had their "cloud-caps on." His wife
saw houses wrapped in secrets.
                              Nobody lives here:

arc, parallel, bisected hill, tan points
beneath blue-metal sky.
                              Nearby, a hostel
built in a monastery kitchen sends its guests
to bed in ovens. Everyone dreams of fire and air.

Everyone dreams of tongues of fire.
                              The children
who mocked as he worked grew arid and repeatable,
a row of black cleft-marks above the road.

THESE AFTERNOONS

They are not, after all, indifferent
to us. They take one another, mingling
like smoke in hair, like a dog's trail-away cry
hanging across otherwise unmarked seconds.

Almost all heat, we too are inseparable
and sit here on the porch of mid-June,
grown suddenly hazy with reticence
about the most operatic of events—

the train at the field's edge hauling itself
to Canada, the butternut tree unfolding
its blue umbrella, most of our skin
naked at last. And we might say

their undulations, their old-fashioned
meanderings through time like a horse
and carriage along a street vaulted by elms,
are like our own deep, if unremarkable, shadows

drifting through a story of love and comfort.
Nothing seems to happen otherwise.
I think you are still pale and beautiful,
and this near-absence of wind, hot

condition of the eyes, these small,
humid rubbings on the arm and cheek,
like sexual breaths, make a long moment,
then slip waywardly through the deep grass.

II

RETURN TO A PLACE
LIKE SEEING

KNOWING THE DAYS

There are eloquent sleeps,
bristling winds, choral oaks,
and the peerless inconstancy
of cats. There are lost days
of nothing but stirring in heat,
like a sail catching stray
puffs. There's an antiphonal
mood, a category like thunder,
that suffers in the impermanent
offing. You must convene
the senses at a suitable remove—
there, say, where the gold flame
pants on its stem—what
a life it makes for itself,
what a pungent share of hunger
it floats up in the guise
of ash! And conduct yourself
after the old prayer. Profess
fraternity to sun, to rain,
deliquescence to lunar
frost. For these are the patterns
of time in an untamed world.
What the body, unconstrained,
is made to remember.

RETURN TO A PLACE LIKE HOME

The empty field below and a haze
along the valley like a fever, thick and achy,

then the horse appears with the sunset wind,
tossing his neck, stamping a little way toward joy.

I live like a window, wait to glitter
or be thrown open to the gaunt cats in the yard.

Together, we drink to the sun, but like theirs
my speech stays in my throat.
                              Outside is the flecked
chatting of women who live with their hearts.

Green shadows fence with the old, raw weather.
Or, I am like the linen belling on the line,

signaling no one, a parched cloud
fallen back toward this straw and shining earth.

CHILD'S EYE

The horses stamp against their shadows,
a hawk glides after its own then circles ahead.

The scarred stone of the house has gone plush in the long afternoon
    light and crawls
from under the blue arms of a pine loaded with cones.

Our neighbor's little girls are naked again,
make mud figurines they'll let dry by the door
and, tomorrow, explain minutely to themselves.

The story of the cat. Of their mother reading herself to sleep
    in the hammock.
Of my fields, the color of their corded hair.
Of the quail they'll hear in their naps that will raise its ruckus
    with the bells.

One cloud like a palm print smears the clear glass of the sky.
A swallow in rondo, mystery, this six o'clock wind, nothing
    getting away.

DAMNED

It was as if the world might leave us alone,
two mad songbirds, to skip on the valley's heavy air
and squeak like nothing spun by the wind.

Because we were damned to no praises, no
requests, no counsel, solitude promised us light.

Poplars shimmered on a little spit of hill, bells
glinted in a spire like a white awl

pricking at God, our one companion, Firefly,
confederate on those hot promenades out
under the arched gate of the moon.
He had us making tiny psalms to the stars.

The fields were rubbing sticks, all whispering grass.
When headlights triangled out of the heat,
we retreated, more shadows, into the blackberry hedge.

Cats rose to us everywhere we slept,
or blackbirds thrashed in the scrolled leaves
until we turned, expecting some other friend—

no one who ever came or who could come
in our long disappearance. There was relief in that,

seeing only the elegant wing, the gold, cruel beak,
nothing, until our dying alone,
that would make us answerable for this life.

PROGRESS

Home to the ever-shifting chair, return
to the same hillside viewed from between every pair
      of listening pines,
the same tanned fields, the same, more southerly sun.

Leaves like green hearts tremble in the poplar
or, yellowed, swirl down the pebbled walk to the hedge.

Here, everything that flies or crawls
stings, but there's a wind in the late afternoon
and voices measuring the progress in the fruit trees.

The young black cat has eyes like a lizard's.
Forever hungry or blooded, he curls near my feet.

I'd ask about the progress of my life,
of the children who'll never run from my hand,
along these crawling shadows, to the far hills and back.

The trees spit themselves down in small, green drops.
The gold bees swing above the grass as if on chains.

I've set the sun squarely behind a pine, watch
as the same ancient sounds return
—the wind-sprawled bells, the cicadas' sizzle and clack,
a call to the mare cantering the field below.

CISTERN

Like deafness, evening muscles in.
Swallows chase themselves in eights around the spire
whose bells swing hard against the past.

The widows misremember each other's past—
to each, each knot of face around the table
was rival in a kindling love.

All summer, they've dined beside the cistern, silver
trembling in their spotted fists.
A small, brown wine beads on the rims of their mouths,

burns half-moons on the linen.
"I loved the children," says each, important as the cloud
in a memory of still water, as the pail rocking in the cistern's arch.

After, their black heels ring the climbing street.
Set in earth with spells, its cobbles leap above the garden walls,
glint quartz, and float back, common, black, dry as day.

"Good night," calls each as shutters clap
against their frames. Inside,
scant light, but faucets hiss like fuses.

MEMORY SONGS

Plain as the purple clover
    or the wind around my knees,
as those little girls fashioning cats
       out of mud, they compose

themselves this Saturday
    in silence and the coming
rain. They're like windrows
       in the meadow, horns

after a wedding, after
    the compromised vows
of two separate terrors. Like
       dishevelings in the garden,

lone farmhouse, spire,
    and riot of caustic engines.
Like the ovoid look of glasses
       in the mirror and the feral,

gray-green curve of jaw,
    notch in the chin for a
symmetry. The brass and nettles
       and joists of every day,

they are as I have sometimes
    refused to accept them,
like summer songbirds, hailstones
       for hearts, skipping around.

TRADE AND TRANSPORT

The borrowed, yellow Vespa that each night
you propped against the horse's
stall—a single, foreign woman
who found here unbridled romance, easy
transportation—remains
where you abandoned it. The horse
still stamps down the hillside, brings back
baskets of figs or the costly, ruby
smoke of fall from the vines.
I think of you back home in a wider bed,
on wider streets, turning
your quick Italian into commerce.
In a few hours you'll see the moon
is jowly, how it spins off wine as stars.
Upstairs, your room's unrented, dark,
the way you kept it, the way, tongue-tied,
restless, I knew yours
even within the nets of dust flung up
whenever anyone approached the farm.
One old boyfriend drives slowly past
the orchard still. Its olive trees
silver in the dusk, their leaves
delicate lips pressed shut.

MOTION NOTES

Siena

Afternoon coffee clears the eyes.
The trees whisk silver all the way
to the vineyard, like wind. Even in the sun,
we could read wrapped in blankets.

Last night, I watched you spinning
your wedding band among empty glasses.
The ring's whirl slowed, broke, chattered down
like a toothless upper jaw.

There are so few birds—pigeon, swallow,
the occasional lark. I read that
whatever else flies, these Tuscans hunt.
The sun flies. It turns brick to plum,
that deep, failing color.

A lizard sips the coffee's rainbowed dregs.
Its sharp head's yellow in the cup.
I flinch. It fires into a crack in the wall.
Whatever moves is the actual subject.
The poplars lean and fidget into night.

ALL THE TIME

Another day of thunder and no rain.
Of exhausted leaves wheeling down
a July afternoon so cool and gray
it could be time for the children to fret
about school. Of the unremitting flow
of traffic returning from the sea.
Each day our landlady, out sweeping
the leaves, threatens to cut down the poplars.
Each day we cry out in fluent alarm,
say how our bedroom seems to swim
in their lights, and she laughs, motioning
to the staked oaks that must grow up first,
and promises, *"Avete tempo."*
Yet we know, by the time they've grown past
our windows, throw their quaking lights,
their slaking shades of green into our sleep,
our bed will be as sand in the room's heart,
we, the graceful contours of wind across dunes.
Last night, in answer to your dream
of being married to someone else again,
I dreamed I kept crying, *"Stavo per,*
stavo per," I was about to, was about to . . .
For we had just returned from a dream sea,
where we'd watched a perfect sky go gray
and close and angry, and when we'd returned,
a man with an impossible accent
was selling ices from the bed of his truck
and honeydews so sticking, so warmly sweet
I knew how all the time we'd ever have
could drift, if not indifferently, away.

HEAT AND CHILLS

The wind has broken away from the sun,
brought the sudden, winkling bells across
the valley, right to my humid hand.
We know the nuns to whom the bells
belong, those ancient, dying sisters.

I lay awake all last night, felt
the moment my legs turned achy
with flu, the moment you came awake
and two roosters imagined light at once.

We say it's never really cool here
and never rains or if it rains
it comes at night and has dried
to bone or ash or bloom by morning.

So that those chills were mine. This damp
on paper. And the green, enameled
flies to whom I taste like crying
or love or witness. So that when you woke,
the sun was set to ignite the sea.

CURRENT

As if the only agency were the wind
and I might let mine, false and patchy, go
into that steady current like a kite!
Certainly, I'd let it take my voice away, dash
what little it showed in the way of wisdom
and lose it, not unmercifully, in the sea's,
in the leaves' cool, quixotic soughing all around.
Each few months I wish again for this change
in the way I speak—more fluently, yes, more
humbly before those I love, but contoured
like this wind riding the shapes of the hills,
bearing lightly down on the valley, the burnt-red
roofs of farms, making over the terraced groves
a precise, immediate, and sweet calculus—
as if what curves over surfaces, stroking
with a feathery hand, knows more surely
the world's throb and corporeal speech. Swallows
dive and squeak, hectic in the windshifts.
There's a smell of rain from the green offshore.
You'd know it in the way the olive trees
whisk and spangle silver on the hills.

LAST NIGHT ON *STRADA DI MANDORLO*

Venus takes the place of sunset,
burns over the thin, peninsular curve of the valley.
The olive trees are gone but make a silver wind
appear in fidgets, disappear in heaves.

It is like an end to candor tonight,
our climbing the Street of the Almond Tree and laughing
to cheer the penned-in dogs, feigning exhaustion
after another day of doing

nothing in the shade. Yet how full that "nothing" is,
like patience, we say (or love),
that hangs on desperately to shadow-crawl, to glances
secretly, or only later caught.

There was an almond tree here once,
a vast, propitious thing like a spell
that cast itself the narrow length of this street
called, then, by another name. I keep

resisting what I have to say tonight—
it would be me. It would be
some thought of preservation or reluctant darkness.
It would be the quiet feeling lonely.

AT THE WEST GATE

Best to leave without ever looking back.
The stone will be the color of coral
and the wind, casting the shutters shut,
ghost-gold, like lemons in a full moon.
There will be wine in every conversation,
over which the smokers linger, let
their forefingers play, enblooding the tips.
Later, they'll press them on the lunar
hollow at the base of their lovers' throats.
You have stamped me that way yourself,
made me your printed card, your indelible
boy, pausing now on the road out, regarding
the abrasive quality of the way, its shells
ground to shard by the endless, sad sandals.
But I have my pack, bread, water, map,
my messages to all the right figures.
They'll be eager to learn, blessed with forgetting.
I can imagine their generous teeth already,
their laughter like choking, like engines
that refuse to start, their profligate eyes
mirrors in the orange zero of the sun.

RETURN TO A PLACE LIKE SEEING

Siena

Things marked in passing:
a gilt mirror surprising me back
to myself, green confections in a window,
breasts, disinterested glances
from those I might once have left.

We arrive under clouds like thin milk,
like advents of rain.
We appear sleeveless again in the doorway.

I could believe what I see
is the same, I could breathe easier.

There are yellow leaves, already some
floating down, one like a great ace.

       *   *   *

At first I see only the hillsides
and the passing of a year
of ashes and more smoke whitening
the sky, the grueling sun.

Two chairs face each other on the sloping lawn.
They are an unequivocal conversation.
They are like what's nourished
by a refusal to reply, by a fine indifference
to being seen.

       *   *   *

I'm like one in a gray garden
who can just smell the heat of day stirring
its ashes beneath the clouds.

The smell of dust on the roses and pages
of a book left on a white chair.
Its words, mirrors of nothing, catch in the leaves
before whispering into the valley.

It is that motion down,
like one's looking over the garden
from the right window, his pencil in place,
that recalls itself in the breath before sleep.

*   *   *

The voice of the day chants
a stone's breath above the earth.

It ends where the wind ends—
at the cool base of the wall,
in the silver-dust sway of the grass,
on the edge of the ocean,
with praise.

The old books of the hours
make promise of bells to ring and a heaven
to reach. Our shutters bang open
on the sun-filled valleyside of the house.

*   *   *

Being so late in the day
and the uncradled wind
feeling at fault, I mind
no one except who comes
calling carrying his question.

Being so late shadows bend
about walls where they serve
to remind me of the death
of the eyes. I keep the versions
of my ears close, earth-

hallowed and singing, close
in thought and the nights echo
more swiftly than the days.
One feels the dark hollow
its heart in the base of the throat.

*   *   *

See how the tall horses
raise the city to life.
They fill the squares with contest
and stones ring in the alleys.

Their same sleekness is the women
in black. The mood is of
the end of convenience. Banners
express an elegant wind.

One has a hand in this
by reflecting the hour.
Concentration comes, towers
its assemblage over the walls.

*   *   *

An indignant, dirty, tangerine light
marks one extent of the mountains
that otherwise fill every edge of our vision.

We were such a long way from here.
Association brought us back, in rain, in wind.

Now the shortened nights have dreamed a fire,
closed the fields in furnace.

There is no meaning to the thought of home
if there is no anger burning in the distance.

                    *   *   *

      There are as many shadows
as days and the bells traverse
        such distance, like carts
rumbling from an earlier, starker century.

      The swallows along the hillside
call monotonously, small
        brown engines that refuse
to turn over, to beat in a sleek oil.

      I'm facing the mountains
of the clouds, red batches
        balancing on the points
of slender trees, precarious region

      where nothing drinks
yet dusty leaves appear
        slick and silver. Who
has shaken out her sack of cotton wisps

      and glint, set them drifting
through all the attention
        anyone could give? The walls,
those ancient Sunday women,

      are powdered white in the heat,
yet what breath there is
        whispers behind the shutters,
promises mountains to be surmounted,

      flames that expect to burn.

*　*　*

So we are casting our eyes down
from a balcony of the afternoon
over a country of vines and tan fields.

The childless life might be a place like this,
an empty stage before which
a vanishing audience whispers
its love affair with the soundless.

A wave from here stirs only a swallow.
We are too far for a glimpse from the road,
and the rest are at work in their kitchens.

*　*　*

Here is not one of the great curves,
one of earth's slowly rolling-away hills,
though it will make an evening-sound
like a bell, like a well swallowing coins.
It's one of the late incisions and tar.
One of a male world's premeditated
scorings, the length of a fast commute.
I've not seen a wind touch just one leaf
of a poplar, not seen the fireflies fill
meadows and do anything but stars.
Yet even here are loved ones who insist
that earth is a woman and their harvest
the least of her mysteries. Who, all alone,
peer between the exhaust-yellow pines
to where the highway and its tiny lights
speed away. Where, coming back,
arrows to home, they vanish under dusk.
And a starling the color of oil slicks up,
a brighter dark in the flickered air.

* * *

Blue is in the economy of love.
It lasts a clear hour then grays above exhaustions
of work, the pure acids of novelty, leaves
only a breeze when it goes.

We watched two great balloons float over
this morning. No one
was hurt but I remembered
a postcard of the city caught from above,
no worse than a queen's face on her coin.

* * *

Before we leave, the gesture must be right.
An available smile and a wondering hand.

We found ourselves not merely
in the cool of the bed but at a table

like regular customers
in slacks and regular chains.

Just when it seems a story might happen,
when it seems the laughter,
the deliberate look . . .

* * *

Not enough branch to sway, enough brick
to amount to a wall,
not enough depth to draw water, light
to spread over the turned earth:

If I had been built instead
from the inside and its pressures out,

42

I might have felt careless,
better enclosed against myself.

There might have been rain and the perfect window,
circling stairs, less deliberate stars.
There might have been shadows like penetrable rooms
so that even grief when it came
would seem intimate and kind.

                    *   *   *

Today takes place what we've chosen
to ignore, to watch
instead a small, uninhabited space beside us
swell in the grim heat.

Despite the work of bells and ten churches,
despite leather and the blue
banner of Mary, who arrives on an oxcart,
despite the dogs howling from barrels,
the gathering shells, the tambours,
and a race run on portable earth.

We refill ourselves with cold wine.
Imagine a beach.
A marble world breezing out over the sea,
the heads of the drowned crowding ashore.

                    *   *   *

The world watches on Friday.
It means to fold you in its arms
like a quiet statue, like rain.
It is what you came back for, why

you may leave. There are birds
who sound like cats, which is like

crying out for the devil of love.
There are cats who wail like time.

A mother who lets her children go
and a highway that bears them off
into the joy of new bodies like hills.
One thing is not just like another.

One thing makes you more and unlike
yourself, as if you were stretched thinly
over the landscape, a fabulous breath
above the hungry grass and its fears.

*   *   *

It's always the light blown off the trees
that's named in the first breath.

The style of just now—brick red, burnt tile—
is a dimension of sun,
what can *be* in the sun for sensible eyes.

The horses wait at the sufferance of the city,
which wants them for their pain.

Saying is not just the means of description.
It's this late afternoon as it occurs, shadow
above shadow, glass on irreparable glass.

*   *   *

I see you are nothing
if not the end of my gaze, its moment of casting
along one possible line
between bodies established so in the dusk.

When the farmer burning the stubble of his field's
first wheat banks the fire against the hill,
smoke fills the valley and flows,
climbing into my eyes.

*   *   *

Next, at last, in this importunate sun, in crow-call
and swollen air, in stunned, bridal afternoon,
and in hours come shadow and the curved,

reclarified fields. So the dear mind
might grow easy, reach coolly into blue space
like the future, like itself in its resistless love.

We nap and listen at the chinks in our sleep—
the cicadas' long-sawing coition,

a finch's singular spark turned array, turned
weft-work and singing, our own breaths
like shadows of leaves poised to brisk in a wind.

Sometimes, summer holds its breath, full of pain,
full of dioxides, of doubt.
Sometimes, in reciprocal blessing, it breathes.

*   *   *

Perhaps that outline of the hills will make
a part of you: this evening, already intelligible
through the poplars marking the meadow's edge,
that smoke, and now the quickened roundel
of the swallows urging the spire to its obligation
of bells, the dampening of dust in the path
like a blue chalk line drawn under moonlight.

Perhaps it all will lose, in drawing you
out to it with down-turned palms, its obstinate,
false depth.
                    Perhaps you'll be as what's visible
sees you, the reflected spark and flicker,
like the lights of water on salt air.

                    *   *   *

One sees the earth he is leaving for home
grow suddenly small and menacing.

He imagines the plane's roar arriving
from far away in the ears of a listener
in his garden miles below, a sound
that refuses to stay local. It fills

an anterior life, shakes the present
from its intentions. It makes
a throbbing no one could mistake for a heart's
alone.

III

THE SAME PLACE FOR TWO

"LITTLE LOW EARTH"

Inhabitations of a phrase by Carol Frost

Not here—unless the phrase occurs to remind you
how any kitchen, any bedroom with a fire
dying at the bedside is a little, slowly cooling
place, like earth;
                  not here—unless by its quiet
disturbance of her poem in which Icarus drops like ice,
you picture ambition, that blaspheming trajectory
under heaven, become now your restless staring
out the window;
                  not here—unless this little,
low farmhouse of mid-last-century stone, built
at the bottom of the land's slow roll through birches,
becomes, in its cooled, conserving darkness, you,
a slabby presence in the look-down of a ridge;

where, in just two days in late October, the sky
has been streams of leaves, then a mysterious backdrop
in which the hillsides group and re-group, against
which the rain-blacked birches arch their particular,
yearning selves, their tremulous, rowing branches;

where, grimacing down the last of some gray coffee,
rain-splatter streaking the panes like leaf-gold
gashes, you take yourself out in the wind.
Follow the stone wall tumbling across the contours
of what was meadow, know that each grown birch

is a day, every leaf a wish that, granted, falls.

RISING SENSE

Today, I vanished in the woods
like a thin shadow. The leaves are back
trembling like dimes, but the first gnats
remind me of dizzy fugitives.

All your life, you said, you waited
by telephones and learned to know the ring
coming from a long way off.
A dryness spread over your palm like a stain
and that meant, Reach for the phone.

I'm waiting for the chance to sneak back,
surprise you at the screen door
like a sprig of laurel in a jelly jar.
I'm waiting for my old self to return.

Sometimes, a wind builds in the trees
like traffic or a clearing fills with moths
like bright mirrors. Sometimes,
there's only sunlight in a blue column
dropping between treetops.

Because you know me so well,
I must have wanted to die.
I must have made this weekend in the woods,
away from comfortable words,
like learning to be gone.

And learning to be gone
has felt like watching beneath another sun,
another color of sunlight,
that stuns the world by its candor.

So distant,
I feel the ground as it changes,
almost imperceptibly,
as if whatever's coming is slight, after all,
or comes from a long way off.

DAY OF SMALL CONSOLATIONS

When I wake, the clouds are like the sky of prairies,
blue-steel and photogenic with snow,
                                    and the wheel-
ruts in the field have crusted over, lost
the hue of yesterday's mud, its glistening, almost
spring-time concern with earth.
                              Probably drifting
clouds passed into my sleep last night,
into its dream of friends slogging through the city's
money, afraid their lives might be richer here.

Someone with a chainsaw's already up and snarling
through the debris of limbs another storm
sent down. One of the street's
                              remembering elms
was split in two, half a perfect trunk, its cream,
unguarded heart whorled and rippled with the imprint
of a gigantic thumb. A little later,
                                    there'll be slanting
snow beneath empty sky, snow and a mid-country sky.
Then the plows will glow inside the dusk outside

and the desperate snow give way to a hard scatter
of stars and farmhouse lamps.
                            And I'll walk today
as I did yesterday, three times around the elm,
pulling for its better half, its upright
half to survive the steel and snow,
                                    kicking
through the chaff and chips of fire-log limbs
to offer to what doesn't need it my own consoling
presence, my gift of two sad eyes, this naked hand,

a surgeon's indifferent concern for the heart revealed.

THE SNOW IS NO MEMORY

as the thaw is not, as the river
drowning the meadow or the pines
slanting behind the church are not.
Bricks squeeze ice from their cracks,
and the slate roofs suffer a kind
of cold that must slicken in sun
to be shed. A room's white lamp
glazes the window where no one
has time, no one watches and waits.
The snow is no memory, as the glass
is not, as I am not, the street
in pieces and the pines almost
black in the gray afternoon wind,
the lampposts quiet and slender,
no child I have ever been, hooded,
sprawled crosswise in a peaked drift.

LAND-HOLDER'S LAMENT

Transience, O seed,
a green-bending river, rain
of morning, fretless medium of will
and failure, low note
like a fan's. Each day
the old man tramps
past the fountain forgetting, boots
slung around his throat,
clothes in fastidious bags,

old pride. I'm appalled to see
how deeds multiply
in my pockets. They must grow
out of disuse, sadness
over my standing. Heart-enthraller,
blond keeper, warm
except in your talons, Sun,
send me away.
This old place

is stumped for ideas.
All its pictures of itself
are mine. Sleep and even
my dreams have labels,
prices, a concordance
of permanent parts. I
can summon any one of them
in a snap, half—as they are—
buried alive.

CIRCLE

Geometrically speaking, we have been
here before. The point at which the line
of our infinite conversation began
its curve, a small, bald premise

in the thicket, clear spot, a respite
on the hard way of confusion, refusing,
mistake, point of a knife's delivering
its deep say-so. Dearest keepsakes:

ring and a prayer, bell and echo,
and the love-round lips; this decade
of the same sky rubbing our eyes
when they open then dropping down,

around the curve of the earth, ending
again where we say—each of us—
"I know what I'm doing," who was
no longer alone and could never

know, being already bent and whole.

6.22.90–6.22.00

TWO, TOWARD TIME

Lack farther, lack faster, lack higher than
the elegant turnings of hawk, lack
ardor, lack devotion, lack
wisdom, care, lack nothing
with its wintry face, stare
and story of wolf and salt and the dead
fall. Sleep of the tongue, rungs
into evening that hums on its back, lack
bearings, lack fruit, lack desperate
grace, space when the next chance comes, confused
in its speaking, bemused
by the house. I have mistaken rooms
in the morning for purity, misled
myself into awakenings like suns. Refreshed
are the bones, the foundling
weeds. Refreshed are the questions
creaking on stalks, are the seeds
and the already poisoned. Refreshed
are the weakened and by this long season
that creeps into mine—like wind,
shadow, like cold,
ghostly face sleeping beside me,
unlike me, wife.

A WATCHING POWER

The gait of memory's slower now.
More than the late summer shadows
has bent toward the meager north.

Slowed, and I find myself, tiny
prophet of discrepancy, watching for
the rust-colored leaves to commence arrival.
I will anatomize the days they stand for.
I will pronounce their briefer value.

Of summer I retain the sparest self.
Only a sparkling edge or, there,
a silky spot I can say and say,
as if fingering lucent cloth, or, worse,

one enormous space, blank with satisfaction,
its corona of blue-gold light turning, sighing.

If I were a saint, I'd say
renunciation welled up from within the choices
granted me, laments made airy silence.

If I were a dinning belly of sickness, I'd know
how shrunken the past must make itself
to allow a present pain its fullest
shouts, its resonant, eloquent
denials of tense. Neither,

I keep clenched, like a chest its plangent heart,
the day-to-day dilating, the nightly contracting
allusions even the body makes
to absent time. I keep them from
some sad sequence they wish upon themselves,
keep them otherwise alive.

I say "I" as one might speak
of fate or dire consequence
having befallen him, as a hail of crows
falls upon the garden. I mean, a watching power
hanging like a catkin out of sight,
out even of the sun, hoping a breath,
a gust might seize it for unforgetting earth.

WANDER

After the innocuous disasters are written,
you should leave time for the silence to return
and wander, stick in your fist, over to where
the plateau of birch and red oak plummets
into a snowy ravine. When the arbitrary effects
are understood, you should wrap your hand
in another's hair, in that silky bandage the color
of the last, sudden slant of a winter light.
You should drape yourself over the arm of a sofa,
over the stair rail, over the outer edge of evening.
Let the blood rush to your eyes as if you were
leaning for a kiss. You should release each hour
and end your long, inventive squabble with faith.
After the days, each day derived from days before,
are spent and explained, you should open the doors
of your house, say the wind threading through
its dispassionate rooms is a new wind, breath
of the curve of the earth, breath of a language
that, reaching, reaching, is impatient to go.

PROMISE

You can hear the Vermont wind
descending—organ hum, ground
of bright fall blue—

long before it comes
shaking the overnight rain
from leaves, tugging at the skin

like restlessness. The wonder is
I ever miss it, appearing so
deliberately within our spare,

rural embroidery of hoots
and gunshots, pick-ups and
the jangle of dogs, loping,

cordial, business-wise. Or
there is such quiet, as now
the world's near absence

makes the mind not mind,
whose several words scarcely
fill their allotted pockets

of breath: as if I were thinking
already of a lowering,
posterior conception, like a noun,

of time and the unintended
ends of summer's slowing growth.
Then wouldn't sleep go coolly?

And aren't those circlets in the road,
leaves, predictable dust, cause
for inattention, inanition?

Descending organ hum,
silence or autumn blues,
I would be that listening in

the well-burnt field and under
its stunted apple tree, prematurely
jacketed and inconsiderable,

your elsewhere approaching
like fact. For you would be
a thing to see, to touch.

You would be a thing to know,
a resolution, distance,
like the resolution of away.

DISCOURSES OF THE RAIN

America is a space filled with moving.
                            —Gertrude Stein

It must matter to our sense of
what's to come that the third mountain
of thunderheads this hour
just grumbled past. We're all lazing
at the bottom of a basin of uncurious
blues, stretching and taking
the spots before our eyes for swallows,
the willow for a hissing,
depthless green. It must matter,
or the season, so frankly distended,
when the rose casts its shadow
of thorn and remote beauty,
won't raise itself above whispers.

        *   *   *

That was that summer ago, noon
when everything felt like bursting
and the ice in a green green glass
slipped famously, its tonic clack
premonitory from here. Now
the air is full of water and
the gentle, burning sound of rain
on leaves. And though once I was
inclined to take such softness
as being's ground, I'm like anyone
traveling through open sky,
tiny now, silent, and so much more
impressed by what disturbs.

        *   *   *

Now all the flood pours down
like one in his hour of
rage, and were it not
for the lack I feel for being
raised in a village without fields,
I'd pray to that coarse,
inclement god. But I'm pious
as a cat, indifferent as glass.
So, no, I won't pray.
Yet neither can I go back:
Devout place—"To Live, To Work,
To Shop"—in whose interest it is
to believe it's under attack.

*   *   *

Money's a coward, the Secretary
says, and he must know, paid
to make the world safe to seduce.
I thought I wasn't, but I'm easy too,
deuce-eyed, nudgeable, various on demand.
Look through me, you'll see the state
of a union. Life's just more
fanatic there, says he,
who promises protection. Before,
there was a drought, mostly on tv.
Now, the rain's with us all the time—
in sideways gusts, in lashing flickers
like nerves in silent movies. Scary.

*   *   *

In rain and smoky thunder we dig.
Eight spoon-sized holes according to the crow,
eight darker shadows to the absent sun.
It was a bargain, eight saplings where

the meadow drops to woods, clenching rock
and one another's roots, commending themselves
to us, our wished-for screen of pines.
Not, of course, for us. For eventual selves,
for whom we wish a place of safety.
At thunder the sky constricts, a little like—
but before—our hearts. Its sepia flares
to nickel and the rain spangles back white
as quartz, as bones that clutch a shovel.

*   *   *

Whoever in the know, whoever else
fingering the sign scored in the metal,
worrying her fingers raw over
the last trace of a testament,
would she cease and into my misprision
whisper what's at the touch of her marvelous
hand. For even my holding the etched
sheet to the sky produces only
a puddle and a winkling as of rain
in the sun. It's not nonsense, not glory,
but survives from a time of troubles.
That much I gather. The date and consequent
hatred are always the last marks to go.

*   *   *

Practical as the rain is,
we hear of it as part of another story—
the old story—of fear and the flood,
of the detritus that arrives,
tarred and toxic, the story of thunder like war
as it rouses us from a low,
dishonest repose.
                    Particular as the rain is,

we hear of it as part of the story that believes
it is the oldest of stories:
how a people who risked the god's anger
lived forever in anger. This
is the short history of the rain as we're told it,
of the rain beating at the clover, sweetly.

                    *   *   *

We're hoping for a break in the weather
to hay, happy at least for the cool wet
and its help at expressing the seed.
As always the world seems to recede
after May, its come-again ceremonies
of commencement and re-hallowing
the dead. Already they look like no news.
I'd like to discover what's constant
in me, to speak of what's uneventful
and nearest the surface, whorled in
my fingertips, accorded only an eye's
discrete blink. It's like a murmuring harbor
here in the rain, like nothing outside.

                    *   *   *

An eloquent day's pent up inside,
a sophist-turned-anchorite bent
in his cave. He's praying to be spared
until Arizona scorches his face
and its flame-made tempests haul
his huskless self to the sun. Fear
inclines me that way too, into
the house, into a creed and its psalms
of indivisible goodness, material
virtue. But the rain says, Find not

a cell, but a raft, for the river
is high and running so fast, faster
ever than its history would hint.

*   *   *

Radio says, Here's the last day
of bruise-green heavens then the sun
will know itself by the meadow's raking
shadows. Two will be ourselves
in branchless, uncrooked transit; two
will be coyote wavering toward blue trees.
Meantime we pretend to read the news
but count the seconds between the lit-up
wind and the thunder concussing nerves.
When the lights fizz out, we wander
the house in candlelight, imagine
easily that century whose medium,
ether, bore light, the lightest name.

*   *   *

If it is as she says that America
is a space filled with moving and
not just the ritual of the crowd,
the timed, daily patchwork on unliving
streets and the conventional wizening
of instinct, then after the rain,
after the rain, under a Friday sun
when the highways are breathing again
and racing to the shore beneath white
pioneers, I see she means how glad
it makes us to forget, that personal
force of headlong wonder, protean
as money, unsafe at whatever speed.

*   *   *

The neighbor's hen chucks like a slowly
squealing spit. It comes down here
on a thick, intermittent breeze.
Fire burns the tinder in the chest
and forehead. The workhorse in the thighs
won't keep indoors. America's war
has just rained fire on a village wedding.
Let's doubt for a moment, may we,
the testimonies of the mind, that foxy
accountant, and stick with what's thistling
the nerves. Mine tell me, be angry,
if unamazed that in such atmosphere
anything, anything at all, will flame.

*   *   *

So hot last night we slept on the floor, let
an old fan's oscillating wind
batter us stiff. There's a filthy murk
already hung over the valley. Up here,
dubious blue, I seem to collect days
like jewels. Like hand-softened tools: hammer,
awl, adze, nickel-fretted plane.
Today, for instance, is going to be for turning
screws, screwing up the pressure so a soul
feels faint. Pointless preoccupation? But
not the only way to make nothing better.
And if nothing as it flames along will be
this century's fact, not the worst.

6.12.02–7.4.02
Heath, Massachusetts

DOUBLE TIME

It is just that hard a thing to
hold on to as June's brief clemency, as
the pure relief of sleep. We step
through the mown grass laid in its bending

windrows, see the moon alone
in the clear sky, in charge. At the seam
of meadow and woods, where the swallows
devise, is a winter of wood to split

and haul, is therapy enough for the cold.
The road is quiet a moment under
a high Canadian wind, its Pacific heart.
A silky laugh comes from farther away still.

And nobody else, to catch this
reticent light on the west-reaching leaves;
no one, our fox, quick and convincing
in a charge of blossom. Almost it becomes

like something we said once and meant
to make last. Almost it's a time so like
that other this straying, this fragrance
of cut green become those transfiguring

words, their hope, our opened secrets.

AFTER HAYING

Swallows dive and snap on long strings,
out early above the just-mown field, its grass and blue
    and russet flowers
already rolled in orange ribbon, those bales
already looking like facts of summer.

Another hour, after a hawk has turned above the edge
    of woods and field
and the ground-holding jets from their base a state away
have brought the next of the troubling clouds—

we'll walk the meadow again,
delighted by the rain, by the way the earth has reappeared
    as hilltop
and curves away all around, passing
from this to another, almost repeatable day.

And tonight we'll watch a red moon clear Burnt Hill
and sail into place, making shadows across the underside
    of clouds,
washing the barn in blood,
                      and so that every day possesses
its own unshared quality—
of observed desire, of cold temporality, of joy,
that wandering, incommunicable motion toward the sky—

we'll stray in place, in fields stripped clean, blade
and wing, our hearts stuttering a little, deliberate, while.

REMINDED OF FORMER HABITS

Till he came upon a web
strung over the strip of yellow,
pitted floor between cupboards:

It had the loose weave
of abandonment,
an air of cumbrous motion,

as in pictures of small things
shown large: A ravel
of dendrites floating

in the gray, fluid space
between neurons, each strand
like a filament of a pale

feather; floating on
the thick ether in some cold
corner, the corner of

geometry or tribal cause
or murder, the corner from which
a small, brown spider,

having set his web
to ensure activity,
vanished, months before.

The strands, too torn and few
to catch the quick,
undesigned flights of thought,

hang till cleaning day
comes with its heavy sponge
doused in ammonia.

REMARKING TIME

The sound of the birch leaves silvering across the meadow
arrives a second after their shudders. Now,
this morning's rain, still working its way through the leaves
 above me,
comes in little, frantic gusts like released steam,
and the ancient apple trees gnarl ever more gladly in the
 thunder-bearing wind.

When the sky turns gray again,
I'll think of revolutions in the weather, of summer uncertain
 of itself
and returning to a season of eager cleansing.

I'll think of what changes as moving as easily back in time
 as forward—
not the way we think of ourselves,
who are becoming more solitary with age,
approaching singularity and a final mood like patience.

Those filaments of a spider's web, stretched between grasses,
go out of focus in the wet, encircling light.

One may never be so remarkable as even that,
yet this change in the weather bears transition's promise:
sky, not-sky, then a cloud-flecked iridescent green and ruby
like quartz, like bad art, so I can say,
I was here for that.

APPLE OF . . .

Two seasons distant and, so, not altogether there,
altogether nothing but the snow-covered hope of a single
    deer, scraping under trees,
the lavish sprays of apples going wild, their greening weight
and blush, blush are now, exactly, mute.

And something I have reached for—ring and tang
and cloud-droplets of concentrated sugar, like rhythm,
    children—
hangs in branches of green wood, dead wood, curves now
    of snow
arching, a vaulted walk-away.

Apple of my sight, apple of a late-August early-evening,
of the first fall mists, the brilliant russet dream of Rome,
    Jonathan dream,
and apple of the night when I remember least and only
    angles, slips
of time and their one cohering color—

you, red mind, sphere and sheer, sweet drop, turned
    in your own time,
fallen like a law, promise of that tip-of-the-tongue
    unknown.

ANXIETY DREAMS

i. 8.8.02

Allowed to get away, allowed to slip back over
    into the savannah lands, the inarable plains
of sleep: the grade-schoolyard girls in haze,

    the dog bite, the belt's crack, teeth
spit in the sink, bitterness evangelized to dust,
    and, blessedly, what's there to say

upon waking without them? I undulate straight
    in here to read the waves and marvel
as the wind scripts its calligraphic way across the leaves.

    Reverdy said, speaking of art,
that the child is presented; it represents nothing,
    as if to its mother, labor expressed in fluid,

shriek, little John wasn't already more and less
    than autonomous good and bed and luck
and several dead family members shown up again.

ii. 8.19.02

I dreamed last night I'd been left again
    so did what souls do . . . went back to school.
Forty and a freshman, hunting for

    the showers, taking instruction from my own
former student (the Korean boy whose blind father's
    a pastor), unfathoming the mysterious,

predictable loss of my comfortable love.
    But, here, I tell you too much, more than
you're wise to know. So let me slip into

a formal frame of mind within
the personal: Intransigent curve, scythe swath,
    unthriving moon seed in phalanx

or dalliance or valance of all possible
    vectors, you are baffled with me this
morning. I'm also dreamt of by the sun.

iii. 8.20.02

After driving away, tearing the handle from
    its hose and the gas pump, he found himself
in the men's wear department of a great store

    unable to locate his wallet, his wife,
or his shirt, so, bare-chested, he wandered the aisles,
    fingering fabrics, tropically embarrassed,

as transparent in loss as he'd wish but never
    dared hope. I woke to the gunfire
of the neighbor kids practicing deer slayer,

    their joyous, pubescent curses a keyed-up
echo of each fresh blast. If I were their father,
    I'd make a run to the whiskey, maybe slit

my tongue on the jagged lip of my favorite
    jelly jar. If they were my kids, disarmed,
they'd have nowhere to go but where their legs took them.

iv. 8.26.02

There was a miner I knew slightly (for this
    was my mother's father) who rode the train
from home to the pit then traveled low

through the roaming tunnels to the anthracite
face, back, practically under his house. Metaphor
    for the dream? No, but perhaps it's like being

a father, out of sight, never far from home,
    as if, when I dream, I dream what I've missed.
So here I am, father and child of my own hard,

    slow-burning fears. Or is it the power
of the father that in secret he undermines
    what he claims to support? Decades later

the unmined coal smolders and the families
    have dwindled, if not all away then to the toughest
remainder, as of his cough to a lifetime of dust.

    v. Labor Day

Last night, for the one time in your life,
    you were all dressed up and alone, leaning
from your parapet over a party, and dancers,

    and glint. When in good fortune and dis-
belief, I came to your side, we were instantly
    discussed, our fancy dress mocked by boys

in khakis and oxfords. "Wear whatever suits you,"
    I retorted, as if in a movie, "then people will talk
and you won't seem so strange to yourselves."

    Labor Day morning and I know what this was:
another back-to-school dream, in which, for once,
    I was kind of a star—eloquent if sibylline,

unruffled, getting the girl. You can't imagine
    how strange this makes me feel, as if someone else
were writing my lines wishing they could have been his.

vi. 9.11.02

I wake to the memory bells in their hollow
    of quiet, wake from no remembered dream
(unless we say the 90s were a dream or a show)

        and listen to the roll call of names on the radio.
A year ago was Day Two of school and now
        we're back at it a week, returning, repeating

ourselves as teachers and dreams and certain sad
        dynamics of history do. On a morning whose date
will henceforth be a code for loss, I think instead

        of what has never been gained, of a boy
of my own, of that love for a son, of a night and a sleep
        of virtual peace disappearing into the cool,

slow daylight of everyday. One bell for one name,
        toll and toll, and I lie awake, certain of what
I'll have for my anxious students to hear.

POEM

Of its forgotten part, its honey,
its hammer, its zone of bud and leather,
of its trial's procedure and delay, those darlings
of the back room, dark room, old shoe
and dry-bouquet keeping room, of
its sidling and falsetto snares, the least
adorned and most despised alike
panting into curfew, returning altogether
blue as beat-up dusk, of its nestling
bed of mica, froth, and ashes where
a further deliberation lies and the bat-
squeaking night rains above, of its furtive,
nibbling style and indecent blotches, of
its twirls and sausage-shaped
redoubts in the hills of home, memory-green
then flaming red to gold to dust
and back, your little lungs surprised,
their intricate tracery chafed, shrinking
a little more, of anything—if you thought at all—
of its iron glamour, of its rind of scholarship,
of its core and bolt and napping promise,
of its design like tarnish on a flask,
like a knot in summer's skein, like shudders—*if*—
then you've thought, too, clear through
to the finale, this, our apprentice song
(of uncharted foolery, of taboo love)
will leave, coldly echoing in the bronze
scoop of an ear, an unshriven, crass rapping
at the door by night, by shivering day.

FAST, FASTER

The grass is haze and a bee
connects the eyes to its curved
green motion sway

down-meadow as if drawn
in the after-air of that jet's
burning through the same

sky in haze in the aural
blear of a chainsaw's nearing
shriek too high for hope too white

like the seventh shade
of humid like no news from the sea
like a fly in the ear the thought

breaks off in whispers in
leaves in the singular
raindrop gone to hail crumbling

cornices rim the hilltop
wall of this day this room
leaking matter my head

lacks air and beats
like the sun I have
to escape only harder the sun

faster sips the little
cups of clover madder the grass
unmoved descends in *S*'s

FIREFLIES

On the gray-green of evening they,
one to other, make signs faint as pearls caught in a mirror.
It's a white inkling, a warm aura they arouse.
He who toils has felt the unaffordable heat.

A moment-longer faces itself in the shimmering glass,
fills with quietest words, most delicate
fears. He would carry them home. They vanish on the way.

The abiding rooms are empty, jealous of such a night,
its vibrancy never again theirs.
Their lamplight is a bandage. Windows blacken willfully.
Who is a ruin knows himself, all history

being now. It seals the least cause in him.
It inhales even the slight, outstreaming breath of ease.
It is not this gray-green of evening, pulsing.

They constellate under a slurry moon, constellate
and vanish into a grayer,
abstracted sky, approach the one thing they could never be.
He sees who has a terrible myth to make.

THE SAME PLACE FOR TWO

If beginning
is slow and white and if
beginning is slow and adheres to the will
like ice on ice, if beginning
wishes the sun to shape its heart
to your eyes, your eyes to the news
a crooked arm's length away,
if beginning waits or, worse, stares
like a man with his own hands to blame
(a sweet man, a sad man, a false,
impersonal man, cat at the window), stares
as the only comfortable room fills
with flame, the excess of song, grim
extent of doubt and unrecoverable
color of stars, as time flows over
his hands, your hands, if
beginning means the same place for two—
this, you, on a corporate shore—
at the limit of change, waiting
for change, change if it could
smile back, the weight of two
the result of beginning, "love,"
and the word turns
like a hand the key in the lock.

NOTES

For their generous advice and unstinting encouragement, I'd like to thank my teachers, in particular Peter Klappert, Ai, Jim Tate, Dara Wier, Paul Mariani, and Roger Weingarten.

"Evidence" is for Ashley Kincheloe Dyson.

"First Stepping in the Deerfield" is for John Marshall and Cindy Callahan.

"Long Shadows" is for Jan and Cal Carr, Betsy Kovacs, and Jack Estes— would that all the green hills and dark valleys be full of Heathens like you.

"Houses by Cézanne" is for Laurie Goddard.

"Little Low Earth" is for Eric Widmer and Meera Viswanathan, who gave us their house and the dream of houses.

ABOUT THE AUTHOR

Born in Washington, D.C., John Palmer has degrees from Duke University, The University of Chicago, and the University of Wisconsin-Madison as well as an MFA from the University of Massachusetts-Amherst. He has taught in Iowa, Wisconsin, Washington, D.C., Amherst, Massachusetts, and Madaba, Jordan. Palmer has had work published in *The Antioch Review*, *Cimarron Review*, *Denver Quarterly*, *High Plains Literary Review*, *Indiana Review*, *Seneca Review*, *Willow Springs*, and elsewhere. He lives and works in western Massachusetts.

Poetry Books from *Pleasure Boat Studio: A Literary Press*

Listed chronologically by release date. **Note: Empty Bowl Press** is a Division of
Pleasure Boat Studio.

Axcendance ~ Tim McNulty ~ $16
The Every Day ~ Sarah Plimpton ~ $15.95
A Taste ~ Morty Schiff ~ $15.95
Hanoi Rhapsodies ~ Scott Ezell ~ $10 ~ **an empty bowl book**
Dark Square ~ Peter Marcus ~ $14.95
Notes from Disappearing Lake ~ Robert Sund ~ $15
Taos Mountain ~ Paintings and poetry ~ Robert Sund ~ $45 (hardback only)
P'u Ming's Oxherding Pictures & Verses ~ trans. from Chinese by Red Pine ~ $15 ~
　an empty bowl book
Swimming the Colorado ~ Denise Banker ~ $16 ~ **an empty bowl book**
A Path to the Sea ~ Liliana Ursu, trans. from Romanian by Adam J. Sorkin and
　Tess Gallagher ~ $15.95
Songs from a Yahi Bow: Poems about Ishi ~ Yusef Komanyakaa, Mike O'Connor,
　Scott Ezell ~ $13.95
Beautiful Passing Lives ~ Edward Harkness ~ $15
Immortality ~ Mike O'Connor ~ $16
Painting Brooklyn ~ Paintings by Nina Talbot, Poetry by Esther Cohen ~ $20
Ghost Farm ~ Pamela Stewart ~ $13
Unknown Places ~ Peter Kantor, trans. from Hungarian by Michael Blumenthal ~ $14
Moonlight in the Redemptive Forest ~ Michael Daley ~ includes a CD ~ $16
Lessons Learned ~ Finn Wilcox ~ $10 ~ **an empty bowl book**
Jew's Harp ~ Walter Hess ~ $14
The Light on Our Faces ~ Lee Whitman-Raymond ~ $13
Petroglyph Americana ~ Scott Ezell ~ $15 ~ **an empty bowl book**
God Is a Tree, and Other Middle-Age Prayers ~ Esther Cohen ~ $10
Home & Away: The Old Town Poems ~ Kevin Miller ~ $15
Old Tale Road ~ Andrew Schelling ~ $15 ~ **an empty bowl book**
Working the Woods, Working the Sea ~ Eds. Finn Wilcox, Jerry Gorsline ~ $22 ~
　an empty bowl book
The Blossoms Are Ghosts at the Wedding ~ Tom Jay ~ $15 ~ **an empty bowl book**
Against Romance ~ Michael Blumenthal ~ $14
Days We Would Rather Know ~ Michael Blumenthal ~ $14
Craving Water ~ Mary Lou Sanelli ~ $15
When the Tiger Weeps ~ Mike O'Connor ~ with prose ~ 15
Concentricity ~ Sheila E. Murphy ~ $13.95
The Immigrant's Table ~ Mary Lou Sanelli ~ with recipes ~ $14
Women in the Garden ~ Mary Lou Sanelli ~ $14
Saying the Necessary ~ Edward Harkness ~ $14
Nature Lovers ~ Charles Potts ~ $10
The Politics of My Heart ~ William Slaughter ~ $13
The Rape Poems ~ Frances Driscoll ~ $13

Our Chapbook Series:

No. 1: *The Handful of Seeds: Three and a Half Essays* ~ Andrew Schelling ~ $7 ~ nonfiction

No. 2: *Original Sin* ~ Michael Daley ~ $8

No. 3: *Too Small to Hold You* ~ Kate Reavey ~ $8

No. 4: *The Light on Our Faces*—re-issued in non-chapbook (see previous list)

No. 5: *Eye* ~ William Bridges ~ $8

No. 6: *Selected New Poems of Rainer Maria Rilke* ~ trans. fm German by Alice Derry ~ $10

No. 7: *Through High Still Air: A Season at Sourdough Mountain* ~ Tim McNulty ~ $9

No. 8: *Sight Progress* ~ Zhang Er, trans. fm Chinese by Rachel Levitsky ~ $9 ~ prosepoems

No. 9: *The Perfect Hour* ~ Blas Falconer ~ $9

No. 10: *Fervor* ~ Zaedryn Meade ~ $10

No. 11: *Some Ducks* ~ Tim McNulty ~ $10

No. 12: *Late August* ~ Barbara Brackney ~ $10

No. 13: *The Right to Live Poetically* ~ Emily Haines ~ $9

From other publishers (in limited editions):

Desire ~ Jody Aliesan ~ $14 ~ **an empty bowl book**

Dreams of the Hand ~ Susan Goldwitz ~ $14 ~ **an empty bowl book**

The Basin: Poems from a Chinese Province ~ Mike O'Connor ~ $10 / $20 ~ **an empty bowl book** ~ (paper / hardbound)

The Straits ~ Michael Daley ~ $10 ~ **an empty bowl book**

In Our Hearts and Minds: The Northwest and Central America ~ Ed. Michael Daley ~ $12 ~ with prose ~ **an empty bowl book**

The Rainshadow ~ Mike O'Connor ~ $16 ~ **an empty bowl book**

Untold Stories ~ William Slaughter ~ $10 / $20 ~ **an empty bowl book** (paper / hardbound)

In Blue Mountain Dusk ~ Tim McNulty ~ $12.95 ~ **an empty bowl book**

China Basin ~ Clemens Starck ~ $13.95 ~ a Story Line Press book

Journeyman's Wages ~ Clemens Starck ~ $10.95 ~ a Story Line Press book

Orders: Pleasure Boat Studio books are available by order from your bookstore, directly from our website, or through the following:

SPD (Small Press Distribution) Tel. 800-869-7553, Fax 510-524-0852

Partners/West Tel. 425-227-8486, Fax 425-204-2448

Baker & Taylor Tel. 800-775-1100, Fax 800-775-7480

Ingram Tel. 615-793-5000, Fax 615-287-5429

Amazon.com or **Barnesandnoble.com**

Pleasure Boat Studio: A Literary Press
201 West 89th Street
New York, NY 10024
Tel / Fax: 888-810-5308
www.pleasureboatstudio.com / pleasboat@nyc.rr.com

How we got our name:

. . . from *Pleasure Boat Studio*, an essay written by Ouyang Xiu, Song Dynasty poet, essayist, and scholar, on the twelfth day of the twelfth month in the renwu year (January 25, 1043):

> "I have heard of men of antiquity who fled from the world to distant rivers and lakes and refused to their dying day to return. They must have found some source of pleasure there. If one is not anxious for profit, even at the risk of danger, or is not convicted of a crime and forced to embark; rather, if one has a favorable breeze and gentle seas and is able to rest comfortably on a pillow and mat, sailing several hundred miles in a single day, then is boat travel not enjoyable? Of course, I have no time for such diversions. But since 'pleasure boat' is the designation of boats used for such pastimes, I have now adopted it as the name of my studio. Is there anything wrong with that?"

Translated by Ronald Egan